The Great
SHEPHERD

7 Promises For Everyday Life Today

TIM L. COX

*Swallow up fears, anxieties, depression and more replacing them
with stability, victory, answered prayer and joy unspeakable!
Know who youa re and what you have in Christ Jesus!*

BOOKSIDE Press

BookSide Press
877-741-8091
www.booksidepress.com
orders@booksidepress.com

Contents

Psalm 23

THE SHEPHERD PSALM

Psa 23:1-6 A Psalm of David. The LORD is my shepherd; I shall not want. He maketh me to lie down in green pastures: he leadeth me beside the still waters. He restoreth my soul: he leadeth me in the paths of righteousness for his name's sake. Yea, though I walk through the valley of the shadow of death, I will fear no evil: for thou art with me; thy rod and thy staff they comfort me. Thou preparest a table before me in the presence of mine enemies: thou anointest my head with oil; my cup runneth over. Surely goodness and mercy shall follow me all the days of my life: and I will dwell in the house of the LORD forever.

INTRODUCTION

What is the Lord? Salvation, life, peace, love, healer, Shepherd and Bishop of our souls, creator of all the universe, assurance, strength, comfort, we could go on and on with all that the Lord is. He is the guide in all our battles, conqueror over our enemies, deliverer in troubled times, He is our healer, our heavenly Father, wisdom, a friend that stick s closer than a brother. The list is never ending, Christ is all in all! (Eph.1:23, Col.1:16, 2:9, I Cor. 8:6) You can know all the Lord is but that doesn't do much good until you get to know Him personally and He becomes my Lord! The Lord is my Shepherd, " I am my Beloveds and He is mine. .. and His desire is toward me! " (Song of Solomon 6:3 & 7:10). The Lord also spoke through the prophet Jeremiah saying , " Thus saith the Lord, Let not the wise man glory in his wisdom, neither let the mighty man glory in his might, let not the rich man glory in his riches: But let him that glorieth glory in this, that he understandeth and knoweth Me, ..." (Jer. 9:23-24).

I want to share with you something that started rolling around in my spirit years ago when my dad went on home to be with the Lord and a few years ago started becoming more clear but was really being revealed to me the last year or two in and about Psalm 23. This Psalm was given to me by so many people when my dad passed which was to help comfort but the Lord started showing me out of this small Psalm 7 promises for everyday life. I started learning more about sheep and shepherds and how they relate to the Lord and us. It has absolutely nothing to do with religion but it has everything to do with relationship. Becoming one with our heavenly Father and Jesus Christ our Lord, the Shepherd and Bishop of our souls! (IPet.2:25). Jesus even prayed that we would become one with Him and the Father and our true brethren as He and the Father are one, (John 17:20-23). I often wondered why this Psalm was mostly used at funerals. The Bible definition of death is mostly in the context of spiritual separation from God. Like in the Garden of Eden when Adam and eve sinned they did not fall over dead but they were spiritually separated from God. They could no longer look Him in the face nor walk with Him in the cool of the day. Holy Spirit departed from them. They were still alive in the flesh but were spiritually dead. When a believer passes on from life in the flesh he is really just changing locations, like moving. Thank God Jesus has made the way for us to be alive in Him again and get the victory here and now and when this life is over we pass on to be with Him forever!

The Bible says we are a three part being. We are a spirit, we have a soul and we live in a body and we our spirit will live forever! To be absent from the body is to be present with the Lord, (II Cor.5:8). God is a God of the living as this Psalm is a Psalm for the living. We must become as intimate with Him as with our husband or wife. We are told in Ephesians 5:22-32 of this analogy of Christ and

His church and a husband and wife. In verse 30 it says that we are member s of His body, of His flesh and of His bones! We should be as close with Him as we are with our husband or wife. This represents a very intimate closeness here my brethren! We must get to know Him better daily. Walk with Him, talk with Him, share everything with Him, He knows it all anyway! Give Him complete Lordship over your life, over your job, over relationships, over your business, over everything! We must become one with Him. He will never let us down nor fail us, He is "the great Shepherd of the sheep "! (Heb. 13:20-21). Remember, being born again we are flesh of His flesh and bone of His bones, we have been made one with Him!

David who is the writer of this Psalm spent much time on the mountains getting to know the Lord while tending the sheep. David saw a likeness between the Lord and His people as with a shepherd and his sheep. When we spend time with someone we grow to understand them and love them the longer we are with them, our bond gets stronger. We need to build this strong relationship with the Lord which will produce strong confidence and trust in Him. This comes by spending quality time with Him in His word and prayer daily. David's confidence, trust, dependency, strength and love grew immensely in his fellowship with the Lord. David spent a lot of time with Him. David learned how to trust the Lord with all his heart, his mind and his strength and his fears and anxieties and needs just as we can through God's word, meditation in God's word, prayerfully being guided by the

Holy Spirit in fellowship with Him! What I want to share with you is seven promises in Psalm 23 that will swallow up fears and conquer anxieties and learn how to trust the Lord and live a victorious life! You will see God moving in your life, be a partaker of His Divine power! Scripture is like food. It must be chewed, swallowed and digested to get nourishment, strength and insight or understanding to alter our thinking which will change our life.

There is no way for a carnal mind to understand and operate in spiritual things and to know the Lord. Romans12:2 says we must not be conformed to this world (formed and fashioned after its mind sets, viewpoints, attitudes etc., Amplified Bible) but to be transformed by the renewing of our minds. We must read, memorize and pray over and be in line with God's word daily to build it into our thinking and to stay in His will and to conform us more to His image daily. We must keep our trust reaffirmed continually in the Lord for each and every situation and circumstance. Jesus said in Luke 4:4 that man will not live by bread alone but by every word that precedes out of the mouth of God.

Peter said that we are born of the incorruptible seed of the word of God (1 Peter 1:23) and in Acts 20:32, it says the word will build us up and give us an inheritance among them that are .sanctified. Feeding on God's word is the bread of life! (John1:1, 6:35). The one and only true, living God that has made all things and has recreated my human spirit, who I am, can surely take care of every area of my life, if I learn to trust Him and follow His lead, getting to know Him more intimately daily and listening to His spirit, in His word.

We constantly want to go our own way , just like sheep wonder off their own way just as Isaiah 53:6 says, "All we like sheep have gone astray; we have turned everyone to his own way ...". We don't know what is on tomorrow, we don't know what is around the corner but our God the Great Shepherd does! That is why we are commanded to walk by faith and not by sight in II Cor.5:7. Going our own way is being led by what we see at the moment , or by what we feel or by what our emotions tell us is right , or taking our own will above the Father's will which is laid out in His word . We must sincerely and truly take our heavenly Father at His word, believe it and act on it knowing that He does know what is on tomorrow. Faith is acting on His word, following His lead. He watches ahead for us just as a shepherd does his sheep. We must stay in Him. So if we need to see an answer, find it in God's word, keep it before your eyes (Proverbs 4:20-23), meditate in it day and night (Joshua 1:8, Psalm 1:2-3) and feed it to your heart for out of the abundance of the heart the mouth speaks.

Jesus said (Luke 6:45). And as we saw in Proverbs 4:23 out of the heart flow the issues of life. Jesus also said in Luke 6:45 that with our mouth we are bringing evil or good to pass. So the mind must be renewed to feed the heart to keep God's word, which is truth, coming up out of our mouths, bringing good things to pass. What a human gives the most of his or her thought life to and talks about the most is what they wind up doing. That is a fact. We must follow Jesus' lead and let Him be our example and pattern for life. We must abide (remain in, continue faithfully in) in Him as He said in John 15:1-8.

Sheep cannot find their own way, they get lost. So it is with us. A sheep when he gets lost he cannot find his way home. So it is with us just as many walk aimlessly through this life, searching, straining and not finding their purpose, fulfillment, peace, joy, true happiness and most of all true satisfying love. They have no true rest. A shepherd provides all this and even more and we have such a great Shepherd, The King of kings and the Lord of lords Jesus the Son of the living God! Many have said "God has given me a mind and I am using it." Well I see in the word of God that yes we are created by God, spirit, soul and body but we were corrupted by sin. It corrupted the mind and the heart, turning from God's will to our own will and we get in mess's and get lost just as sheep do. We have a Shepherd to guide and to keep us. It is an absolute that we must have our mind renewed to the Lord's way. David knew the Lord and he knew his covenant he had with the Lord and this confidence built great strength in David's inner man. True strength that overcomes in victory and any obstacles in life come from inside you. That is where you are born again, Christ in you our hope of glory! (Col.1:26-27}.

David conquered the world in the strength of the Lord! When all of Israel was trembling with fear because Goliath the giant was taunting and cursing them, David the shepherd boy stood forth and said " ... Who is this uncircumcised Philistine that should defy the armies of the living God?" What he was saying is this man giant or not does not have a covenant with God but we do so why are you so fearful and have no faith? David qualified the battle right there and determined the outcome. David was not moved by Goliath's size nor was he moved by Goliath's harsh words from his mouth. David knew his covenant with God, His heavenly Father and he knew who he was in Him! All of the army of Israel saw a man too big to defeat, David saw an opportunity for God to glorify Himself! Is there anything before you that seems too big to defeat? Problems, finances, health, situations that look to far gone to straighten out, etc.? We have a covenant established on even better promises (Heb.8:6) through our Shepherd the Lord Jesus Christ! He knows the way, He knows the how and has all strength and power to do it! (Phil.4:13, Matt.28:18) God gave David the strength and the ability to deliver the lamb out of the lion and the bears mouth and he smote them and said this giant Philistine will be as one of them, God will deliver him into my hand and God did!

David went to Goliath with his staff and his sling. David looked Goliath in the eye and told him" ...I come to thee in the name of the Lord of Hosts, the God of the armies of Israel whom thou hast defied. "And David took out the giant, David delivered Israel that day through the power of God! (Read I Samuel 17:1- 51 emphasis on verses 26, 32- 37 & 43-47)

Believing that God knows us and really does care for us not only eternally but also here and now is sometimes difficult for the human to comprehend. But the fact is that He does and Jesus is our Shepherd, for Jesus said in John 10:11 "I am the good Shepherd". He will lead and guide our every move in this life right on up to the time to pass on and then He will take us home To these ends I want to bring this shepherd Psalm of David to light for our present everyday life. Notice the word is in verse one is in the present tense, it is in the now. The lord is my _ Shepherd. From here we will explore how the shepherd and his sheep relate to our Lord and us and look into seven promises through Psalm 23 that will take us from fear and worry to faith, strength and victory in God! Psalm 23 is the John chapter 10 of the Old Testament.

Psalm 23

1. The Lord is my Shepherd, I shall not want. 2. He maketh me to lie down in green pastures: He leadeth me beside still waters. 3. He restoreth my soul: He leadeth me in the paths of righteousness for His name's sake. 4. Yea though I walk through the valley of the shadow of death I will fear no evil: for thou art with me: Thy rod and Thy staff they comfort me. 5. Thou preparest a table before me in the presence of mine enemies; Thou anointest my head with oil: my cup runneth over. 6. Surely goodness and mercy shall follow me all the days of my life: and I will dwell in the house of the Lord forever.

My prayer is that this book will encourage you and strengthen you as you let the Holy spirit reveal these truths to you for a strong and victorious stand in our Lord Jesus Christ as we walk this life in Him, Jesus Christ is Lord, The Great Shepherd and our heavenly Father will be glorified by Him and through Him!

CHAPTER ONE

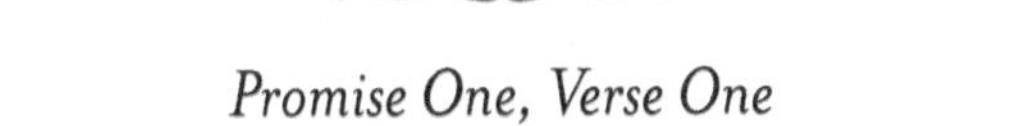

Promise One, Verse One
"The Lord is my Shepherd; I shall not want."

THE LORD WILL WORK IN MY BEHALF.

Our life in Christ is not necessarily our work for Him but it is in us allowing Him to work in us, through us and for us. God said in Ephesians 2:8-10 that we are saved by grace through faith, it is the gift of God, not of works but He went on to say that we are His workmanship created in Christ Jesus unto good works. Like what Jesus said in John 14:10 "... the Father that dwelleth in me He doeth the works." And so it is with us as sons and daughters of the most High God! In the beginning God formed man out of the dust of the earth and breathed the breath of life into him. God put His very own life into Adam and he became a living soul, he became a god- man. God gave him dominion over all the works of His hands for God said let them have dominion over the fish of the sea, the fowl of the air and over every creeping thing upon the earth and Adam literally became the god of this world (Gen .1:26,28), until Adam and Eve bowed their knee to the suggestion of satan. We see then they experienced death which was spiritual separation from God and satan became the illegitimate god of this world, as Adam handed it to him. We know this by Jesus temptation on the mount in Luke 4:6-7 where satan said "...for that is delivered onto me and to whomsoever I will I give it." Also in II Corinthians 4:4 he is called the god of this world who blinds the minds. Now sin has entered in and we have a deceiver constantly tempting us with the lust of the eyes, the lust of the flesh and the pride of life and the cares of this world to keep our eyes off God and get our faith level down and in that our trust decreases, then worries and fears set in. To many times people (Christians) seem to have more faith in the problems abilities to harm them than they do in faith in God to overcome them. This must be true because otherwise we would not worry. You cannot worry in faith and Heb. 11:6 says it is impossible to please God without faith. Worry is the fear I mentioned. It is meditating on the lies of the devil and the world rather than meditating on God's word and building an inner image based on God's Word instead of based on the problem or the situation. That is why the children of Israel did not enter into the land that God had promised them (See Numbers 13:17- 14:38). Meditating on the problem will get you nowhere. We need to meditate on the promises of God and get victory. Glory to God, He set in motion a plan in Genesis 3:15 to redeem or purchase us back out of satans hands, out of the world's way, out of the kingdom of darkness to be translated into the kingdom of Light of His dear Son Jesus! When we are born-again we become ''Christ-men'' (Christians) just as

Adam was a "god-man" before his fall. And we have been given the Holy Spirit to keep us, empower us and hold us until the final part of our redemption. He comforts us, He guides us and He teaches us, He and Jesus are one! Sin corrupted our hearts and minds. We don't always see the best ends and we get ourselves into messes. We must look to Him just as sheep look to the shepherd. Sheep eat and graze and do not see that the pasture is running out but the shepherd is always looking ahead for more and better grass and good water. Sheep are not smart and neither can we see the best ends, as Proverbs 14:12 says, "There is a way that seemeth right to a man, but the end thereof is the ways of death. We have to have divine intervention from God by the new birth and indwelling Holy Spirit to walk in that abundant life Jesus came to give us,(John 10:10b) I Corinthians 2:16 says that we have the mind of Christ , the very thoughts, intents and purposes of His heart through His Spirit that lives within us that teaches, guides, and directs us as we feed upon His word and meditate on it day and night that we may flourish, be successful and prosper in all that we do just as we are told in Joshua 1:8 and Psalm 1:2-3. We must be spiritually minded and worship God in spirit and in truth (John 4:24) and this comes through meditating in the word. Jesus see's ahead and is constantly watching out for us if we will just continually look to Him. Hebrews 7:25 says that He ever liveth to make intercession for us. Who else is working full time in your behalf? To know that you know that at this very moment, in this day, in whatever might be confronting us, our Shepherd is working for our welfare constantly. There is nothing else at all that can set us free from fears and worries than knowing Him and His care for us .Jesus said know the truth and the truth will make you free. He is the truth, the way and the life! Colossians 2:9-10 says that in Christ Jesus dwells all the fullness of the Godhead in bodily form and we are complete in Him who is the head of all principalities, powers and the rulers of the darkness. Verses 13-15 say that we were dead in our sins but now we have been made alive in Him and He has blotted out the hand writing of the ordinances that was against us, that was contrary to us, He took them out of the way and nailed them to the cross. He spoiled the principalities and powers that had any grip on us and made a show of them openly, triumphing over them! Death is now swallowed up in victory!

Jesus is the head and we are His body. All things have been put under His feet, which is under His body which is us ! Now in the name of Jesus, through Jesus we have that authority back over satan and all evil and dark forces of this world! (Ephesians 1:19-23). We are more than conquerors through Him! (Romans 8:8-37). We have been given the full armor of God to stand against the wiles of the devil and the sword of the Spirit which is the word of God to cut him down! (Ephesians 6:10-18). Why is it then we still get anxieties and fears and get anxious and worried? Because just as sheep we tend to think we can find better pastures, we want our own way too much, we resist the plans of our Shepherd and do things our way instead of

His. A lot of the things might even seem good or right in our own eye or even do many of them in the name of Jesus asking God to bless our plans instead of sincerely searching Him in prayer to find His plan which is blessed.

Philippians 4:6-7 says, be careful (or anxious) about nothing but in everything by prayer and supplications with thanksgiving let your request s be made known unto God. and the peace of God which passeth understanding shall keep your hearts and minds through Christ Jesus. Continually looking to Jesus in prayer and the word we will be continually conforming to His image, putting away bitterness, aggravations and any unforegiveness which keeps us from God's blessings and blinds our minds. We must look at people and things through His eyes and His love which is far above ours. He is our Rock and mighty fortress; He leads us and guides us for His names sake (Psalm 31:3-5). We must do it His way without compromise. Proverbs 3:5-6 says " Trust in the Lord with all thine heart and lean not to thine own understanding, in all thy ways acknowledge Him and He shall direct thy paths." When you know Him, you will trust Him as a sheep does his shepherd and you will be a bold, victorious witness to the presence and power of God in this world! Know the truth and the truth will make you free (John 8:32). Worry has never changed anything but the worrier.

Worry causes stress on your body and can actually make you sick. And you cannot worry in faith. Worry is the opposite of faith and remember that Hebrews 11:6

says it is impossible to please God without faith and Romans 14:23 says that anything that is not of faith is sin. Worry believes more in the ability of the situation or circumstance hurt you, it is meditating on the lies of the devil, more than meditating on God's ability and power to overcome them. Every day is a new day, a life full of surprises. We are to forget yesterday and reach forth to those things that are before, pressing toward the mark for the prize of the high calling of God in Christ Jesus! (Philippians 3:13- 14). Jesus said in Mathew 6:33 for us to seek first the Kingdom of God and His righteousness and all these things would be added unto us. What things is He talking about? "All things that pertain to life and godliness!(II Peter 1:3-4). Don't worry about tomorrow for tomorrow will take care of itself Jesus said in Mathew 6:34. So let's keep our eyes on Him and follow His lead and live today for all we can and tomorrow will be taken care of and your yesterdays will always be good memories. He knows what is on tomorrow we don't.

I like what brother Dave said the day we spent the whole day in Psalm 23, about a little boy who apparently had to memorize the 23rd Psalm for Sunday school and he got the words mixed up and said "The Lord is my Shepherd, I don't want anything else ! " That is how we should be! That is a personal relationship as a new bride waiting for her husband with yearning and anticipation. This should be the true meaning and heart cry of us all. When we know the Lord and know that He is my Shepherd, we will not want for anything. We will have entered in to a personal relationship with Him and be free from religion and it's ideas, creeds, rites and rituals. Dave told us another story about two men in church that stood up to quote this Shepherd Psalm. The first was a great actor and the second was a little old man. The actor got up beautifully and eloquently quoted the 23rd Psalm. Then the little old man stood and repeated it and silence fell on the whole place. After the moments of silence the actor stood up and said "I know the Shepherd Psalm but this man knows the Shepherd!" You can tell someone that has this personal and intimate relationship with the Lord. You see it on them and hear it in their voice. They have a boldness about them and a warmth and a glow that only comes from the Lord. Can you say I know Him? Have you ever said, Lord, I need You more than I need anything else? That kind of relationship will put you over in the cleft of the rock, will put you in position for healing, for having all your needs met, an abiding in God Almighty with Whom nothing is impossible! This personal relationship is available to all and the Lord yearns for this with each and every one of us. We must make that conscious choice and decision moment by moment of each and every day to yield totally and wholeheartedly to Him in our whole life and livelihood. We shall not want for anything when we know Him. He is our Shepherd and He will guide us down life's path, victorious in the physical realm and in the Spiritual realm!

CHAPTER TWO

Promise Two, Verse Two
"He maketh me to lie down in green pastues:
He leadeth me beside still waters."

THE LORD WILL PROVIDE FOR ME.

He leads us to what we need if we just follow His lead. He leads us day by day in all circumstances. Getting up in the morning, spending time with the Lord in prayer and His word He prepares us for the day. the more I think of how sheep are the more I understand this Psalm. I had heard much about Jesus as a Shepherd and us as sheep but never really knew much about sheep until we studied about them and it is really something of the likenesses there is. Sheep can be very restless, just as we get restless in our minds and emotions when they are focus on the things of the world and the flesh or self. Only sheep that are taken care of, or are full or content lie down and rest easily. They move about with confidence. Green pastures and still waters describe what the sheep need and want. This is why David said "He maketh me to lie down in green pastures and leadeth me beside still waters." He was actually saying that, He has fed me with exactly what I need, I have knowledge of

His presence and I am content! I Timothy 6:6 says that godliness with contentment is great gain. The Amplified Bible uses such words as "a source of immense profit" and "a sense of inward sufficiency" to further describe the blessed Holiness we are to walk in with Him!

This brings many other scriptures and promises up in my spirit. First being that the Lord said He would never leave us or forsake us (Hebrews 13:5). Jesus told us in some of His last words before His ascension that He is with you always even to the end of the world (Mathew 28:20). We need to build an inner image of that inside us and build it into the fabric of our thinking until we don't just read it or quote it but until we know it to be fact and rely on Jesus daily in all circumstances and things we do. He is Lord, He is my Lord so everything that concerns me or everything that I do must be filtered through Him. Then I start receiving perfect peace, yes I said perfect peace which is another promise from God to us in Isaiah 26:3 which says, " Thou wilt keep him in perfect peace whose mind is stayed on thee: because he trusteth in Thee. " When we have that peace inside, our minds start to function more properly and we will be able to see the best ends to a situation, questions ect. And how to get to those answers and secure them. It all comes through Him! Jesus has been made wisdom to us(I Corinthians 1:30, Colossians 2 :3) and we can do all things through Christ Who strengthens us! (Philippians 4:13). With that perfect peace we as sheep can be content, we can lie down and our sleep will be sweet (Proverbs 3:24, Psalm 127:2). We will start seeing the power of God manifesting in and around us, our bodies even get healthier (Proverbs 4:20- 22).

We are told in Philippians 4:19 that "My God shall meet all your needs according to His riches in glory by Christ Jesus." When we became born-again we confessed Jesus as our Lord, we made Him Lord of our life, in other words we gave Him free reign over our lives. This means every aspect of our lives. He is very interested in our jobs, our relationships and every part of our life and being. We become a new creation in Christ Jesus, a new creature! (II Corinthians 5:17). We are no longer strangers but fellow citizens of the saints and of the household of God, Of whom the whole family in heaven and in earth is named! (Ephesians2:19 & 3:15). If we are in Christ then we must keep our affections set on things above, (Colossians 3:1-3). As we do He will be meeting all our needs here in this life, here and now just as Mathew 6:33 says "Seek ye first the kingdom of God and His righteousness and all these things shall be added unto you." David said in Psalm 37:25 that he had never seen the righteous forsaken nor his seed begging bread. We must simply trust Him and continually follow His lead. The Lord is always looking ahead for more green pastures and quiet, still pools of water to drink from. Sheep will not go near fast moving water. When the sheep's wool is long they can get weighted down and drown and so it is with men in the fast pace of this life, the cares of this world and all our human selfish ideals of what life is all about and what we are to do. We get caught up, we get our self in places that we don't know what to do and so we to can get weighted down and drown in the rivers of life. Jeremiah 10:23 says the way of a man is not in himself. Our hearts and minds were corrupted by sin, therefore man turned into himself. Looking to himself for answers.

The fall of Adam was literally a fall into himself. He went from God's will to his own will. Proverbs 3:5-6 says to trust in the Lord with all your heart and do not lean to your own understanding but in all our ways acknowledge Him and He will direct our paths. Isaiah 55:8- 11 says that His thoughts are higher than ours and His ways are higher than ours and He sent His word to prosper in us. His word is His thoughts and commands for us to feed upon. We must put His thoughts (His Word) in us, meditating on them day and night and keep them coming out of our mouths. Then we are promised to be like a tree planted by the rivers of water that flourishes and brings forth fruit in all seasons! (Psalm 1:2-3, Jeremiah 17:8).

I do not understand all His ways but I know that He loves me and He will always guide me down the right paths and all my needs will be met as long as I continue to follow His lead. I don't worry about tomorrow because I do not know what tomorrow holds but my Lord Jesus does know and He already has fresh green pastures to graze in and the clean, clear, still waters to drink from lined up! Psalm 119:105 says His word is a lamp onto our feet and a light unto our path. We must stay in His light lest we fall into the rushing waters or the cesspools of life, We must be Holy and concentrated wholehearted to Him, following Him at all times and then we will be peaceful and content in this life no matter where we are at or what the situation is just as sheep are with green pastures and still waters.

I Timothy 6:6 says that Godliness with contentment is great gain so let's stay in His word, applying it to our life from our heart for it is forever settled in heaven! (Psalm 119:89). Everything He said is still true, His word is still alive and powerful l and every promise is for us through Christ Jesus as II Corinthians 1:20 says, all the promises in Him are yea and in Him Amen unto the glory of God by us! In other words all His promises are yes and so be it! Malachi 3:6 says that God never changes, He is still the same today so let's let Him lead us daily moment by moment to green pastures and still waters, joying and beholding His order as we live in love, peaceful, prosperous, content, joyful and victorious, today and forever! Hebrews 13:8, Jesus is the same yesterday, today and forever!

CHAPTER THREE

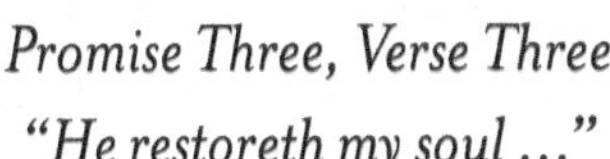

Promise Three, Verse Three
"He restoreth my soul ..."

THE LORD WILL KEEP US GOING.

Are you ever or have you ever been "downcast"? The term comes from sheep husbandry. A down cast sheep is one who has rolled over onto his back for some reason or another, maybe has fallen in a ditch. Downcast is being in such a condition that one is unable to roll back over and get back on one's feet. When sheep fall like this they cannot get back up on their own nor can they get up by the help of another sheep. They have to have a shepherd. Sheep left in this position for approximately five hours will die. If the shepherd does this up righting correctly it is a very tender process. The shepherd must lift the sheep up and rub the sheep's legs until he is able to stand because the blood has drained from the legs . What does this mean to us? Do we ever fall? Do we ever get our self in a mess? Do we ever stray from our good Shepherd Jesus, by going our own way, doing what we think is right? Do we ever let the cares of this life and the burdens of this world weigh us down? How about depression or aggravation? Our Shepherd Jesus Christ can and will upright us in all! Trials and tribulations will come in this world but Jesus said be of good cheer because He has already overcome this world (John 16:33) and the Amplified Bible in that verse adds "... [Take courage; be confident, certain , undaunted!] For I have overcome the world. [I have deprived it of power to harm you and have conquered it for you.] And I John 4:4 says that greater is He that is you than he that is in the world! What we do in and with the various situations determines our growth and many times determines the outcome. The Lord will get us back on our feet. We do not have to stay down. All of us at one time or another have felt like a failure and have had fears and worries. Fear of the past, fear of the future etc. We tend to want to hit our self or kick our feet just as the downcast sheep. Then comes our good Shepherd and picks us up right where we are. There is nothing impossible with God. 1Peter5:6-7 says to cast all your care on Him. Worry is lies of the devil and activates him just as faith or trust in God moves Him. Faith is the only way to please God Hebrews 11:6 tells us. So trust and follow God's lead and don't faint in your mind, keep your eyes on Him! We are a three part being, we are a spirit, we have a soul and we live in a body. Our spirit (us, who we are) is what is recreated in the new birth but our soul area is the mind, will and emotions still needs to be renewed or saved by the engrafted word and James 1:21 says that our soul is saved by receiving the ''engrafted word''. The word engrafted in the Greek means implanted. So we are to implant God's word in our minds that our will and emotions turn from our own to His as we continue to feed our hearts which overflows strength to yield our bodies to the Holy Spirit. As we yield our bodies to the Holy Spirit He gives us the strength to bring our body (the fleshly desire s and temptations, mind sets and emotions) under control and submission to God to live a holy and pure life and keep us righted.

Sheep follow lead very well. The problem is that it is not always the right lead. They are enticed easily and so it is with us. It is easy to get off track and follow the ways of the world if we don't keep our eyes on Him at all times, following His lead. Jesus said in John 10:27 that His sheep hear His voice and follow Him and back in verse 4 of that chapter He said that His sheep know His voice .So by planting God' s word in ourselves the Holy Spirit starts witnessing the word, giving us insight, understanding, revelation and guidance in all that we do, (Johnl4:26,16:13).

II Corinthians 4:4 says the devil is the god of this world that blinds the mind so if we are guided by our natural affections, the world's way or the worlds order of things, of which is a carnal mind, will and emotions we will get led astray. James 4:4 says that he who is a friend of the world is an enemy of God and I John 2:15- 17 says that he who loves the world does not have the love of the Father in him. Isaiah 56:3 says that we all like sheep have went astray and have turned everyone to their own way. That is why we had to get born- again and we must govern our lives and actions according to God's word. It must become alive, powerful and active in our everyday life. It will change us and everything around us. The saving of our soul or the restoring of our soul can be the saving of our whole being, spirit, soul and body, temporarily now in all situations and circumstances to eternally! Our minds cannot save us, that is mental ascension. Believing with the whole heart is what saves us as Romans 10:9-10 says if thou shalt confess with thy mouth the Lord Jesus and shalt believe in thine heart that God hath raised Him from the dead, thou shalt be saved. People live and conduct their life by what they truly believe in their heart. The mind is like the goal setter. Think of a thermostat on your wall. It is a goal setter. You set it on the temperature you want your home to stay at and as long as the power is on and hooked to the furnace or power unit - that power unit will work constantly to keep the goal of the temperature set on the thermostat. We must keep likewise keep the goal setter set of our mind by intake of the word of God to keep feeding our heart, if we don't we can faint in the mind and therein cut off the feed of faith to the heart. Our mind, will and emotions must be renewed or restored to God's word and guidance in order for us to function properly in all the affairs of life. God is the one who created and designed us and everything and He alone knows how to keep everything going. If we don't we will be spiritual beings in a carnal world with a carnal mind, living after the sin nature and be totally ignorant to our covenant with God and how to truly live and walk with Jesus. Everything starts in the spirit realm and you cannot figure out spiritual things and problems with a carnal or worldly mind. That is why a lot of people have such a problem with getting out of addictions or depression, they are trying to fix a spiritual problem in a humanly way and it just does not work, it does not last. Ephesians 6:12 says that our fight is not with flesh and blood but with principalities, powers and rulers of the darkness and spiritual wickedness in high places. We must let Him restore our soul by receiving His word, being renewed by it and acting on it in our everyday life. John 1:1 says Jesus is the word and in verse 14 that the word became flesh and dwelt among us. 1 Peter 1:23 says when we are born again it is by the seed of the Word of God! You cannot have Jesus without the word and you cannot have the word without Jesus. The written word gives faith to the unseen word (Jesus) who is sitting at the right hand of God continually making intercession for us! We must take Him at His word and act on it just as we would the word of our lawyer, our doctor or our very best friend etc. David said in Psalm 107:20 that He sent His word and healed us and delivered us from our destructions. And Jeremiah 1:12 says God watches over His word to perform it! We need to quit kicking and fighting within ourselves and completely rest in His grace. Labor to enter into His rest, Hebrews 4:11. We are to fight the good fight of faith not fight everything else. Again in I Peter 5:6-7 we are told to humble ourselves under the mighty hand of God and cast all our care on Him because He cares for us and He will exalt us in due time. The God that created the heavens and the earth can create and fix any situation of ours. Sheep are not for carrying burdens and neither were we made to carry burdens; they came with the burden and toils of sin passed right on down from Adam. Jesus bore our sin on the cross and in that was all that was affiliated with it. Isaiah 53:4-5 says He bore our grief's and sorrows just as much as He was wounded for our transgressions, iniquities and healing! Hallelujah!

When the pressure of life is on, we need a touch from the Lord. One word from the Master, our great Shepherd, will still any storm in life just as Jesus literally stilled the storm in Mark 4:39. Stand still on the word of God in faith, believing and watch the glory of the Lord! Jesus said in John 11:40 " ... said I not unto thee, that if thou wouldest believe, thou shouldest see the glory of God?" It is only when we back off and have doubt that the worry and fears come in. That is when we have turned aside by putting our eyes on the situations and off Jesus. Peter walked on the water on Jesus's word "come" until he took his eyes off Jesus and looked at the wind boistress, that is when he started sinking, Matthew 14 Lets keep our eyes on Jesus and keep everything in our life under His name, His blood and His control.

Sheep stay very still when the shepherd is shearing them because the shepherd knows the pressure points and has complete control and so is our Lord the great Shepherd in complete control. So let's be still in Him and not limit Him as Psalm 46:10 and Psalm 78:41 says in the KJV.

God wants us to relax in Him when the pressure is on. It is our choice how we react. Pressures do nothing but make one old and sickly. It is a known fact that the majority of sickness and ailments are directly connected to worry and deep grief. Sheep need that constant daily touch of the shepherd and so it is with us . We must be in touch with our Shepherd Jesus Christ daily, growing to know Him more intimately, loving Him more and conforming more to His image.

Problems? Give them to Jesus now and let Him restore your soul! He is waiting. He is very interested in our families, our jobs and every aspect of our life. To confess Jesus as Lord means just that, that we have made Him Lord over every part of our life and being, we have given Him complete control. In any and all things He will get you on your feet and going without fail! Christ Jesus has been made unto us wisdom, (1 Corinthians 1:30), we have the mind of Christ (I Corinthians 2:16). Glory to God! He will fix, renew and give vibrant and abundant life! Only Jesus can upright you!

CHAPTER FOUR

THE LORD WILL GUIDE ME.

Isaiah 53:6.says that we all like sheep have went astray, everyone turning to their own way. Jeremiah 10:23 that the way of man is not in himself, that it is not in man to direct his own steps. And again in Isaiah 64:6 the Word says that all our righteousness is as filthy rags. There is no way we could make our self clean or pure in God's sight. Sin is in the flesh and the world but yet Isaiah 43:7 says that everyone that is called by His name is created for His glory! There is the key, "created". Ephesians 2:10 says we are His workmanship created in Christ Jesus unto good works. When we are born-again we are brought from death to life, from unrighteousness to righteousness. II Corinthians 5:21 says Jesus was made to be sin that we might be made the righteousness of God in Him! Now His very life dwelling in me has given me the desire and the power to do what is right in this life. We have to let Him work through us, guide us and make our way. How does He guide us? BY the Holy Spirit who witnesses and gives us revelation of God's word, through prayer and through other Spirit filled Christians and even some circumstances. God's word is so very important. He instructs us by and through His word. The paths of our life discussed in the pages of the Bible, (God's word to us), are the paths that all believers should desire to be led and kept by and not to turn aside from them. It is those who walk in these paths that are led to those green pastures and still waters.

As Isaiah 32:17 says it is the work of this righteousness that brings peace and the effect of this righteousness is quietness and assurance forever! I'm sure we have all been guilty at one time or another of trying to justify our self by our own goodness, hard work, etc. but the fact is we cannot earn what is already ours. We must release our own will and look to His will and then we are in a position to receive this free gift and then we can depend on the Lord to guide us. Jesus said in Mathew 11:28-30 for us to come to Him and He will give us rest; To take His yoke and learn of Him, His yoke is easy and his burden in light. We need to follow closely the life of Christ, give our self to Him and put to death the deeds of the flesh (Romans 8:13, Colossians 3:5-10) and get renewed to His way in all of our ways and things will work. We are even commanded to walk as He walked in I John 2:6. We must let Him work through us to achieve this. We must yield our bodies to the Holy Spirit for this power (Romans 6:11-18).

The Bible speaks of righteousness in two ways. One

way, the main one is being in right standing with God, which Jesus did through His death, burial and resurrection from the dead. And then there is living right, doing what is right here and now in our everyday life which is out of love flowing from our recreated spirit, acting on and living by the living word of God. We must pray and look to Him for guidance in all that we do no matter how big or little a thing it might be. Making Jesus the Lord of our life means that we now belong to Him.

1 Corinthians 6:19- 20 says we, our body is a temple of the Holy Spirit, a temple of the living God, we are bought with a price, now glorify in your body and spirit which are God's. I John 3:7 talks about he that does righteousness is righteous even as he is righteous. I see this as we yield ourselves to the Holy Spirit to give us the understanding of what is right and the power to live it. We will be practicing what is right according to the word and the more we practice it, walk in it, the more we will be conforming to the image of Christ Jesus!

What has been recreated in our inner man will be manifesting in an outward appearance in our life, actions and conduct. Proverbs 13:6 says righteousness keeps him that is upright in his way and Proverbs 14:34 that righteousness exalts a nation! God loves them that follow after righteousness, Proverbs 15:9. Remember that Isaiah 43:6 said we are created for His glory! And again in John 17:10 He said He is glorified in us! We are called by His name, so if we yield our whole being to Him, spirit, soul and body He will guide us in all the right ways which will be very well for us in this life here and now and this will glorify Him in the earth for His names sake, Hallelujah! We cannot loose following Him! Psalm 119:105 & 130 refers to God's word as light. I John 1:5 says that God is light so as we walk in the light of God's word we are walking in Him and the blood of Jesus cleanses us from all unrighteousness (I John 1:5-9). We walk in light, love and life! I believe this is a highway of holiness that takes us through the wilderness of this present world, in victory in every area of our life just as Isaiah talked about in Isaiah 35:1- 10, emphasis verse on verse 8. Peter told us we are to be holy as God is holy (I Peter 1:15- 16). Being led of His Spirit we can do this. We will receive the power when the Holy Spirit comes into us as we are told in Acts 1:8. This is why the indwelling Holy Spirit is so important Jesus said " ...It is expedient for you: that I go away; for if I go not away the Comforter will not come unto you; but if I depart, I will send Him unto you." (John 16:7, see also John 14:15- 17,26, 16:13, Acts 1:8, 1 Corinthians 2:9-16).

John the Baptist in making the way for Jesus and baptizing, told the people that Jesus, Who was coming, would baptize with the Holy Ghost and fire! We need the fire of God in these days to burn out the worldliness in us! We know that on the day of Pentecost in Acts chapter 2 the Holy Spirit came into His earthly ministry and cloven tongues like as of fire sat on their heads but also Jeremiah spoke of the word of God like as of fire (Jeremiah 23:29, 20:9). That God's word was as a burning fire down in his bones he could not let go of! We must have that fire of the Holy Ghost in us to keep us holding on that tight to God's word to burn out the impurities and worldliness in us and to walk in the power and the love of God in this life. The Lord, through His eternal Spirit will keep us on the right path in this life as the sons and daughters of the Most high God! Romans 8:14 says he who is led of the Spirit is the son of God and again in II Corinthians 6:18 He said I will be a Father to you and you will be my sons and daughters! We will be led down the paths of righteousness for His names sake! Praise Jesus! See also Ezekiel 36:20-27.

CHAPTER FIVE

Promise Five, Verse Four and 1st Part Verse Five
"Yea though I walk through the valley of the shadow
of death will fear no evil; for thou art with me Thy
rod and Thy staff they comfort me. Thou preparest a
table before me in the presence of mine enemies :...

THE LORD WILL PROTECT ME.

Have you ever walked through dangerous places? Have you ever had difficult experience or difficult situations? How about this present world we live in where murder, rape, drugs and violence is on the rise and sin is snowballing. As the redeemed of God we have been delivered from the power of darkness and He has delivered us into the kingdom of His dear Son Jesus! (Colossians 1:13). We enter into our heavenly citizenship when we are born again (Ephesians 2:19-22, 3:14, 20 & Philippians 3:20) and we have become partakers of His divine nature escaping the corruption, moral filth and decay (2 Peter 1:2-4). He has given us His strength and might and His full armor to stand against the wiles of the devil and all the principalities, powers and rulers of the darkness of this world and spiritual wickedness in high places (Ephesians 6:10-18). The angels are ministering spirits sent to serve those who are the heirs of salvation (Hebrews 1:14).

David knew very well that the angel of the Lord encamps round about those who fear (reverence) the Lord God and they deliver them! (Psalm 34:7). I always thought the valley of the shadow of death was talking about physical death as we know it, as we understand it in the flesh but it is in fact a portion of road between Jerusalem and the Dead Sea or the Jordan river at the north side of the Dead sea,   which is called "The valley of the shadow of death". David traveled it much. It is the portion of road described by Jesus in the parable of the Good Samaritan in Luke 10:29-37 where the man had fallen among robbers and thieves and was robbed and beat up and left for dead. This was a treacherous and dangerous portion of the road in which villains would hide in wait for their next victim. Violence and wickedness ran rampant as they lurked in the shadows behind the rocks waiting for people to pass through to ambush them. Sounds like an old western movie doesn't it? That is how it was. Is it so much different today as crime, violence and drugs are running rampant in our city streets and even moving into the suburbs? No, it is no different, people, sin and violence are the same today, the only difference is that is growing worse.

People seem to look at people back then and think "What heathens" and they think that we have advanced so in technology and live in such an advanced society but the fact is these were spirits driving people back then and when they passed on the spirits took up residence elsewhere, just look at the news. Spirits do not die. They are the same evil spirits influencing people today. They have learned to move in the negativeness of the world as their father the devil. 2Cor.4:4 says that the devil is the god of this world and 1John 4:5 says if we have the same view point of the world then we are of the world being under the influence of the world, which is being influenced by the wrong spirits. The present world we live in flows in this negative influence. Being born again by the blood of Jesus we should strive daily to conform to the Lord's way because we should be living in His economy. Our fight is not with flesh and blood it is in the spirit realm (II Corinthians 10:35 & Ephesians 6:12). We need to be just as aware of God's presence and delivering power today as David was when he wrote this Psalm. God is the same today as He ever has been, He never changes! (Malachi 3:6, Hebrews 13:8). We must study His word and spend time with Him in prayer to come to an understanding of who we are in Christ and get that inner image built inside you of who you are in Christ Jesus and what is available to us today for our everyday life.

Jesus said in Mathew 28:18 that all power both in heaven and in earth has been given to Him and in Colossians 2:9-10 that in Jesus dwells all the fullness of the Godhead and that we are complete in Him Who is the head of all principalities and powers! Everything starts in the spirit. It is a spirit that influences people to do the things they do whether it be the Holy Spirit unto holy living and righteousness or to all the spirits of the forces of darkness of this world and of the devil to unholy living and unrighteousness and wickedness. Therefor we must deal with them in the spirit, we are slaves to which ever we yield to, there is no in-between, you are being influenced by one or the other all the time (Read Romans 6:1-23). We must deal with all things in the spirit. Isaiah 41:10-13 God tells us to "fear not" because He is with us with the right hand of His righteousness. Jesus is the righteousness of God, seated at His right hand and Jesus said "... I am with you always even unto the end of the world (Mathew 28:20) and again in Hebrews 13 :5 " ... I will n ever leave you or forsake you." I John 4 :4 tells us that " ... greater is He that is in you than he that is in the world! Jesus has been given all power in heaven and in earth and a name which is above every name of things in heaven, things in earth and things under the earth and that every knee will bow to Him (Philippians 2:9-10). We are seated in heavenly places in Christ Jesus now! (Ephesians 2:6). All this to here is enough to shout and dance about but there is more! His rod and His staff that comforts us are instruments of authority. Mosses carried one, David carried one and on down the line. The staff could be used as a powerful weapon or the hook to pull a new born up to his mother to nurse, to help guide in the right direction. Either way both instruments were used for support. If a new born sheep would get into the hands of a human the mother would then reject it from nursing because of the scent that would then be on the new born. In this case the shepherd would take a dead sheep from the same group and skin the hide off the dead sheep's back and lay it over the new born and the mother would then take it back in to nurse. Immediately I see a parallel. Isaiah 64:6 says all our own righteousness is as filthy rags and Isaiah 59:2 that our sins and iniquities have separated us from God, they have hid His face from us but Glory be to God He has clothed us with the robe of righteousness! (Isaiah 61:10). Jesus, was made to be sin for us that we might 'be made the righteousness of God in Him, Praise the name of Jesus! (2 Corinthians 5:21).So put on Christ as we are told in Romans 13:14, put on the new man, which after God is created in righteousness and true holiness! (Ephesians 4:24). We are joint heirs with Christ! (Romans 8:17). We are carriers of His name, His Holy Spirit and His word in this earth, we are His anointed ones, we are the body of Christ in this earth! In I Corinthians 12 the apostle Paul talked about the gifts of the Spirit and that they are manifested in different members of the body, the body being us, he used the human body as an example. All of the true born again believers make up the body of Christ and Jesus is the head. Thinking of this parallel, do you ever send your body to the store, or to work or to anywhere else without your head going with it? Of course not that is silliness! It cannot be done. It is foolish to even think something like that. Well so it is when we are born again, blood washed children of the one and only true living God in Christ Jesus! Psalm 110:2 was part of the prophecy of Jesus the Messiah coming and the Holy Spirit there called Jesus "the Rod of thy strength" .The strength and comfort that is for us and we start to see the apostle Paul talking about this strength we have here and now in Christ. "And what is the exceeding greatness of His power to us ward who believe, according to the working of His mighty power which He wrought in Christ when He raised Him from the dead and set Him at His own right hand in the heavenly places, far above all principality, and power and might, and dominion and every name that is named, not only in this world, but also that which is to come: and hath put all things under His feet and gave Him to be the head over all things to the church which is His body, the fullness of Him that filleth all in all ." (Ephesians 1:19-23). We are told in II Corinthians 12:9-10 that in our weakness His strength is perfected, to glory in infirmities that the power of Christ may rest upon us and the Amplified Bible adds "(yes, may pitch a tent over and dwell upon me!).

All through the gospels we see all demonic and evil spirits fleeing at the rebuke of Jesus and we have seen why, because all principalities and powers, all things have been put under His feet! We are His body so that means all things have been put under our feet as us being His body, the church! This is the mystery, Christ in you your hope of glory and that these would be made known to all principalities! (Colossians 1:26-27 & Ephesians 3:9-10). We must get the inner image of this built inside us and stand in His strength and boldness in this life. I John 4:4 says "...greater is He that is in you than he that is in the world." Greater is Jesus in us than any of these things in the world! He lives in us, we have even been given God's full armor! (Ephesians 6:10-18). And we have the angels and ministering spirits to serve and protect us, (Hebrews 1:14, Psalm 34:7). And we have the power, teaching and guidance of the Holy Spirit residing in us! No wonder the apostle Paul said the Lord is faithful Who will establish you and keep you from all evil (II Thessalonians 3:30 and the Lord will deliver me from every evil work (II Timothy 4:18). And John said that whosoever is begotten of God keepeth himself and the wicked one toucheth him not,(I John 5:18). In other words, fear not I am with you says the Lord! God has always said it and is still saying it! We must abide in Him, love Him with all our heart and walk in His ways. We must keep ourselves in Him, working in unison with Him. Follow His lead, He will lead us and guide us every step of the way when we are open to His direction and protect us in this dark world all the way!

We will have green grass to graze in in the midst of danger, in the midst of this crooked and perverse world. We must take His way in this wicked world and He will feed us and hold off the enemies. This table prepared before our enemies has to be in this world because we have no enemies in heaven! God said He wipes away all tears there, there is no more pain, no suffering, no sickness, no more crying and no more dyeing! So glory to God according to this He has made plenty of provision for us here and now and to keep us for that final redemption! "For whatsoever is born of God overcometh the world and this is the victory that overcometh the world even our faith." (I John 5:4).

How many times has the Lord saved you from destruction? Saved you from impossible situations? Saved you from danger? Saved you from depression? What is on your table? The Lord will keep victory, strength, love, joy, peace and wisdom on it! What we have to do is " Trust in the Lord with all thine heart and lean not to thine own understanding, in all thy ways acknowledge Him and He shall direct thy paths." (Proverbs 3:5-6). See, it is when we do acknowledge Him in everything we do, in all our ways that He then directs our paths, so don't ever back off of faith, trust and have full confidence in Him. Don't be satisfied with a few crumbs on the floor, get up in the chair, scoot up to the table and fear not for God has the full course prepared for you!

The staff was also symbolic of the Holy Spirit. The staff had three uses. One use was for guiding the sheep. Sheep ranges were referred to as tables. The shepherd would always guide them to good grass (good tables). Number two, the staff was used to lift the new born to the mother. And number three it was used to catch an individual and draw him in for a close examination. Thank God our Shepherd goes before us in every situation! The Holy Spirit which is called the Spirit of Christ (Romans 8:9) will teach us all things and will bring all things to our remembrance what Jesus has said and will show us things to come (John 14:26 & 16:13). Jesus also went before us in death as we know it in the flesh so that we can draw close to it in confidence and with joy. He has swallowed up death in victory, He has the keys to death, hell and the grave! (Isaiah 25:8, Revelation 1:18). And He is very able and willing to take us from this very moment all the way through our life in this present evil world in victory daily and then on to victory with Him afterwards! Jesus knows every pain, every sorrow, every grief and every temptation. sin, sickness, demons and fear must flee at the presence and name of Jesus! (Isaiah 53:4-5, Galatians 1:4, Hebrews 4:14- 16, Psalm 91:10-11, Philippians 2:10). "The law of the Spirit of life in Christ Jesus has made me free from the law of sin and death (Romans 8:2). That is now! that we may boldly say with David when something does try to come our way "Though I walk in the midst of trouble, Thou will revive me; Thou shalt stretch forth thy hand against the wrath of mine enemies and thy right hand shall save me . The Lord will perfect that which concerneth me: Thy mercy oh Lord, endureth forever ..." (Psalm 138:7-8).I will walk this life in confidence, I will fear no evil as I walk in this evil world because God is with me and in me, His Rod and staff (Jesus is the word and Spirit) comforts me and protects me and my way is prepared, even in the presence of my enemies. Glory, honor and all praise to our great and mighty Shepherd, the Lord of lords and the King of kings, our Lord and Savior Jesus Christ!

CHAPTER SIX

Promise Six, Last Part Verse Five
"Thou anointest my head with oil; my cup runneth over."

THE LORD WILL HEAL ME.

The healing ministry of the shepherd was a very important one. The shepherd always healed the sheep of all ailments. One in particular I want to talk about is flies. Summer time is fly time. People who have had much to do with livestock know this can be a serious problem. There are many kinds of fly's, the warble fly, the blow fly, the face fly, the heel fly, the deer fly and the nose fly, just to name a few. The summer months could be a time of torture in dealing with the nose fly. Nose fly's like to put their eggs in the sheep's nose, it is moist and warm, a perfect breeding ground. In a few days the eggs hatch the worm like larva and they go right up into the sheep's head. This causes intense irritation and severe inflammation. When this happens the sheep try to find relief by beating their head against trees, rocks, posts or anything they can find. Even if the sheep do not have the larva inside them they will become frantic, filled with fear and panic just being aware of nose flies around. At the first sign of the fly the shepherd would mix up an antidote made of oil, tar and sulphus mixed together and he would apply this oil to the sheep's head. Once it had been put on, there would be an immediate change in behavior, an immediate relief from the irritation. All aggravation and restlessness was gone! This is an exact picture of irritations in our life. Whether they be distractions, problems in family, personal or business situations, or just an uneasy mind.

Not sure of something? How about aggravation, bitterness, sickness or disease? What about alcohol, drug addiction or depression? Do you have any nagging distractions in your life? Jesus is the healer! Peter pretty much summed up Jesus' ministry in Acts 10:38 where he said "How God anointed Jesus of Nazareth with the Holy Ghost and power Who went about doing good and healing all that were oppressed of the devil; for God was with Him". Jesus never refused anyone. He said in John 6:37b that "... him that cometh to Me I will in no wise cast him out. "Everywhere you read in the gospels He always brought healing, restoration and good tidings of the kingdom of God. All you have to do is believe in Him and receive Him by faith. That true sincere faith and belief will change your life, attitudes, actions and conduct, to follow Him, to live a Christ like life. Sin came in at the Garden of Eden and along with sin came decay and sickness in the world. Many diseases and sicknesses are found also in the curse of the law in Deuteronomy chapter 28. Galatians 3:13 says that Christ have redeemed us from the curse of the law and II Corinthians 5:21 says that He was made to be sin for us and so because of this

I see all through the scripture a redemptive process to bring us back to a whole being - spirit , soul and body. The apostle Paul even prayed we would be kept, all three parts, blameless until the coming of the Lord, he prayed our whole being! (1 Thessalonians 5:23).

Any depression, oppression, sin, sickness or disease is under the law of sin and death and Romans 8:2 says that the law of the Spirit of life in Christ Jesus has made me free from the law of sin and death! Verse three says He condemned sin in the flesh and verse six says to be spiritually minded is life and peace. Jesus paid the price for all, He paid the price for everything on that cross and was raised for our justification! Verse eleven says that if the Spirit of God Who raised Jesus from the dead lives in you, your flesh will be quickened, that is made alive! Jesus sent the Holy Spirit. The Holy Spirit came into His earthly ministry the day of Pentecost and is indwelling believers who are born again in Christ Jesus and is still working the same today Praise God!

We must have the Spirit of God to understand spiritual things (I Corinthians 2:9-16). He brings power into our life (Acts 1:8). All through the Old Testament we see the anointing of oil on a person representing the Holy Spirit. Actually the oil was symbolic of the Holy Spirit and in many cases of a person being anointed we would read of the Spirit of God coming upon them. Men were always being anointed for the service of the Lord. A good example of this is David being anointed (I Samuel 16:13). All things of the Old Testament were shadows of the realities to come in Christ Jesus. There is now an indwelling of the Holy Spirit, a baptism in the Holy Spirit if you will. I do not want to get into any doctrinal beliefs, teachings or debate or anything like that. I only want to say what scripture says.

Baptism or baptize in the Greek literally means to "submerse". What history says of this word is that it was used of die makers, the ones who would die garments to different colors. They would put the garment into the bucket or pot with the die in it and soke it, completely submersing it in the die and then when they would take it out of the pot it had completely taken on the color or characteristic of the die. In other words it took on the identity of the die. Can you see the parallel? We are to put on Christ and walk in His Spirit (Romans 13:14, Ephesians 4:24, Galatians 5:16, Romans 8:13- 14). The scripture also says in Galatians 3:27 " For as many of you as have been baptized into Christ have put on Christ." So when we are born again and walking in His Spirit we are living a Christ like life, not because of anything that I or you can do but a continual yielding to the Holy Spirit to take on Christ's identity. Just as the submersed garments in the die would take on the identity of the die color so we being submersed into Christ, in His Spirit (baptized in the Spirit) will take on His identity! The Holy Spirit is the agent of the new birth, we are birthed through the Spirit. Jesus used the term "... born of the Spirit ..." in John 3:5. Jesus talked of a baptism in the Spirit, an endowment of power to witness and live a Christ like Holy life to walk in His power! In Mark 1:8 it is called a baptism. Jesus words in Acts l:8 said that they would be baptized with the Holy Ghost not many days after that and we know that is what happened the day of Pentecost in Acts chapter two.

Then we see Peter going to the gentiles and them receiving the Holy Spirit just as they did on the day of Pentecost (Acts 11:16- 17). This is still going on today. We must have the Holy Spirit indwelling in us for guidance and power today just as then. The church of Jesus Christ is still going today. Jesus said that it was for our good, it was to our advantage that He went away so the Holy Spirit could come and He would abide with us forever (John 16:7, 14:16). It is through the Holy Spirit that we mortify the deeds of the flesh and live a holy, consecrated life, conforming to the image of Jesus like we are supposed to (Romans 8:13). Holy Spirit brings life and liberty! Jesus said in Luke 11:13 that if you know how to give good things to your children how much more will He give the Holy Spirit to them that ask Him! Jesus knew we have to walk in fellowship and obedience with the Father for us to really live in His blessings and His moral laws and the only way for us to do this is to have His power in us, we cannot do it ourselves. He said ask for the Holy Spirit and He would fill us! Then the oil of the Spirit flows within us healing and giving life. The Holy Spirit brings peace to the mind for we have the mind of Christ (I Corinthians 2:16) and we must have Him to know how to operate in that and the power to submit to it.

Just as one anointing of oil to the sheep was not enough for the whole season so we need to ask for fresh fillings at different times and in different situations. This is backed by the New Testament, especially the book of Acts.

What fly is bothering you or tormenting you? Wrong thoughts, jealousy, lust, bitterness, unbelief in some area, negativeness? Ask the Lord to apply the oil of the Holy Spirit to your mind! Yield yourself to Him and let Him work in you. Line up your mind with God's word. Hebrews 11:3 says the worlds were framed; they were made by the word of God. Hebrews 1:3 says that all things are upheld by the word of His power, God's word and John 1:1 says Jesus is the word of God and in Colossians 1:15-16 that by Him all things consist!

God's word is His creative power so let's Keep His word coming out of our mouths, speaking in line with Him, keeping our minds stayed on Him. Isaiah 26:3 we will have perfect peace when our minds are stayed on Him. The apostle Paul also said in Philippians 4:8-9 to keep our minds on whatever is true, whatever is honest, whatever is just, whatever is pure, whatever is lovely and the God of peace would be with us and guard our hearts and minds and that we would have the peace of God that passeth understanding in verse 7. There is another disease common to sheep also. Summertime is also scab time. Scab is a highly contagious disease, it is a microscopic parasite. This is also found around the head .Sheep love to rub heads in an affectionate and friendly manner. Here again we find the treatment or anointing of oil mixed with other chemicals. Today vats are used to dip the sheep in. The most difficult part of this is to do the head, it must be forced under.

This brings even more parallel. We are very easily swade by what we see and hear. The mind can become contaminated in this perverted world. We need here again to be transformed by the renewing of our mind (Romans 12:1-2) and be governed by the word of God and the Holy Spirit and be not yoked with unbelief as it says in II Corinthians 6:14-18. We must be a light to the world, to all people but be careful not to depend on the worlds systems, it's viewpoints and ways. We need to abide in God's economy which will override the natural circumstances when stood in by faith. We need to listen to the Spirit of God and not the news. We need to spend time with brothers and sisters in the Lord and not with the worldliness. It is easy to get into negativeness or bitterness etc. when we spend more time in the things and conversations of the world's ways than with the Lord, His word and Godly people. It robs faith and Hebrews 11:6 says it is impossible to please God without faith. According to II Corinthians 4:4 the devil is the god of this world so we must give ourselves a living sacrifice to the Lord and be not conformed to this world but be transformed by the renewing of our minds (again see Romans 12: 1-2). This transformation by the renewing of our mind comes through the word and meditating on it through the Holy Spirit, yielding ourselves to Him for the wisdom and power to apply it to our lives and live it out in holiness. Our head does not always want to accept all that is in the word as for today because of the contamination of the worldliness in it but just as the sheep get immediate healing and relief so do we by giving our self to Him. This complete dipping in the vats of oil makes me think again about complete submersion in the Holy Spirit. We need to have that wholehearted commitment to Him. Once we do make the decision to let go and completely submit to Him - mind, will, emotions and body big changes start taking place, life becomes full and vibrant!

When the oil of the Holy Spirit comes in us, our life is in control because it is then controlled by God. A lot of religious leaders do not like it just as a lot of them didn't with Jesus in His days on the earth but this is only because they do not have control. When God has control things happen. When men will not yield completely to the Spirit of God they take control out of God's hands doing it their self all in the name of God but it is nevertheless their move and not God's and therefore many get in wrecks spiritually and physically and bondages are open to set in . When God has free reign in our lives and in our services things happen, love flows without grudging, that ''agape'' , unconditional love flows, people get born again, families get fed and restored, people get healed and set free from bondages of the world and sin. We will bear the fruit of the Spirit as it says in Galatians 5:22-25 which is love, joy, peace, longsuffering, gentleness, goodness, faith, meekness, and temperance. We become one with the Lord! Jesus is our healer spirit, soul and body. According to Acts 19:1-6 there were apparently believers there that did not know that there was more to get after the new birth but Paul told them and they received the infilling of the Holy Spirit.

There are many things that belong to us that many are unaware of or have been taught that it is not for today but that is religion talking and not God. He said in Malachi 3:6 that He is God and He does not change and again in Hebrews 13:8 that Jesus Christ is the same yesterday, today and forever! In II Peter 1:3-4 we see that we have been given all things that pertain to life and Godliness!

Ask the Lord now to fill you with His Holy Spirit! Jesus said it would be like rivers of living waters flowing out of your belly! (John 7:37-39). Here we find our cup running over, a cup is a portion of those living waters that flow from the throne of God! They flow out to others, that is our portion running over. Our life becomes so full of His life that it can't help but to overflow. Ezekiel spoke of a river that flowed from under the door of the temple in Ezekiel 47:1- 12. This river flowed continuously and the waters healed everywhere they went. They nurtured and flourished everything they touched, they gave life! Jesus Christ is the door (John 10:9) and anyone that drinks of His water shall never thirst again, he will have a well of water springing up to everlasting life! (John 4:14) And these will have rivers of living water flowing out from inside by the Spirit of the living God indwelling inside us! John said, this He spake of the Spirit! (John 7:3-39)

Hallelujah! Glory to God! Back in the passage in Ezekiel 47 it says the river got deeper the further he went. The further it goes the deeper or fuller it grows and so is the path of the just Proverbs 4:18 says, it is a shining light that shineth more and more unto the perfect day! Water is a life giving source. It also cleans and refreshes. The water that flowed from Jesus' side on the cross was part of the formation of the church, which is called His bride and in Ephesians 5:26 it refers to the word as water to wash and cleanse His bride the church. The word of God washes us as we study it and meditate on it and prayerfully apply it to our daily lives. This washing of the water by the word also sanctifies us as Jesus said in John 17:17. There are many storms of life that try to muddy the water or stir it up in a tempest but Jesus calms the storms and purifies the waters. One word from our great Shepherd will calm any storm! He is alert to everything that is approaching, every obstacle, interference trial or temptations so stay in Him! Keep yourself under the anointing at all times! "For all the promises of God in Him are yea and in Him Amen, unto the glory of God by us. Now He which stablisheth us with you in Christ and hath anointed us is God. "II Corinthians 1:20-22.

CHAPTER SEVEN

Promise Seven, Verse Six
"Surely goodness and mercy shall follow me all the days of
my life: and I will dwell in the house of the Lord forever."

THE LORD WILL PURSUE ME.

This is another bold statement of David's assurance in the Lord. How many believers can naturally say " I am being followed by goodness and mercy" 24 hours a day, 7 days a week in no matter what occurs in their life? On the hill tops and in the valleys? It is easy to say when all is going well but what about when times are tough, the death of a loved one, jobs fold up, no money to pay bills, or friends turn against you? Yes, He is still there! We need to keep our eyes off the cares of the world that choke the word in us (Mark 4:19) and keep them on Jesus! We walk by faith not by sight (II Corinthians 5:7) and faith comes by hearing the word of God (Romans 10:17) and Jesus is the author and the finisher of our faith! (Hebrews 12:2). To know His goodness and His mercy is to know Him. To know and be able to say with confidence "The Lord is my Shepherd!" Even when I miss it, I am being convicted of my wrong. The Lord is pursuing me. I ask forgiveness according to I John 1:9, look to the Holy Spirit for the power not to do it again and the power to keep going with Him and grow from it. When we are truly in Christ we will glean something good from everything that comes our way, whether good or bad, in all circumstances if we handle it in Him. Jesus said in John 16:3 "These things I have spoken to you that in Me ye might have peace, in the world ye shall have tribulation but be of good cheer, I have overcome the world." He has already overcome the world so stay in Him, (we are more than conquerors) and be of good cheer!

It is the times that we believe we can do things better on our own that we mess up. Thank God He doesn't ever give up on us! We must learn what we truly are and have when we are in Christ. Our life is hid with Christ in God (Colossians 3:3). There is no difficulty that can arise without some good coming out of it as long as we stay under His lead. James put it this way, "My brethren, count it all joy when you fall into divers temptations; knowing this, that the trying of your faith worketh patience. But let patience have her perfect work, that you may be perfect and entire, (lacking) wanting nothing. " (James 1:2-4). Patience in the Greek is being consistent, be consistently constant at all times knowing that God is with you and is pursuing you with His goodness and mercy. God inhabits the praise of Israel, (His people) it says in Psalm 22:3. Praise stops the enemy and stills the avenger! (Psalm 8:2). Praise God that His goodness and mercy does follow you all the time in everything. It is when we handle all the affairs of life in Him and His way that we will see this goodness and mercy following us and know that all things work together for the good to them who love God, who are called according to His purpose (Romans 8:28). We see in Romans chapter 8 again He is talking about the Holy Spirit.

When we are living and walking in the Spirit there is nothing the devil or the world can throw at you that will not be turned around for good through the power of the Holy Spirit if you handle it all in the Holy Spirit by the word of God in the name of Jesus! Look back over your life of something that might have happened that you trusted the Lord for guidance and deliverance, when it was totally in His hands it came out to your benefit didn't it? Could have been to benefit someone else even! Jesus really does know what is best.

In tough times great foundations of faith and unswerving confidence can be built if we only handle everything in Him. People start seeing you as stable and reliable and no matter what goes on you are the same in every situation and good always comes out. People see this and it is a testimony to the goodness and power of God. His goodness and mercy follows you! You are leaving a good trail behind! Think about it, the goodness of God leads men to repentance (Romans 2:4). So I think of it this way, what do I leave a trail of, sadness or gladness, pleasure or pain, peace or turmoil, forgiveness or bitterness, love or hatred, lack or prosperity? As I said before Jesus life can be summed up in one verse, Acts 10:38, How

God anointed Jesus of Nazareth with the Holy Ghost and power, Who went about doing good and healing all that were oppressed of the devil. Stand steadfast in the Lord at all times expecting that goodness and mercy to be following you.

I've heard it said and have seen it true that the atmosphere or expectancy is the breeding ground for miracles! God honors steadfast trust, confidence and expectancy. A good example of this is found in the book of Daniel where Daniel's three friends Shadrach, Meshach and Abednego (Daniel chapter 3) would not bow to the image the king erected, even after being threatened to be thrown into the fiery furnace. Verse 17 says, "If it be so, our God Whom we serve is able to deliver us from the burning fiery furnace and He will deliver us out of thine hand O king." And in the next verse we see the deep, true attitude and devotion and love for God those three had, verse 18 - "But if not, be it known unto thee 0 king that we will not serve thy gods nor worship the golden image which thou hast set up." These boys stood on God's word, they trusted fully in the Lord. This is unwavering trust in God Almighty! As you know they got thrown in the fiery furnace and in verse 27 it says the fire had no power over them! The Lord Himself was seen walking in that fire with them and walked them right up out of that fire with absolutely no harm or hurt on the whatsoever! The king made a decree after this that no nation or peoples speak anything against God because of all this! (Verse 29).

Think of what God can and will do when we totally yield our bodies and whole beings to Him through the Holy Spirit! We are to do all things without murmuring or complaining because we are lights that are to be continually shining bright in the midst of this crooked and perverse world and we are to hold forth the word of life! (Philippians 2:14-16). The Lord goes with us confirming the word with signs following (Mark 16:20). Jesus Christ is the same yesterday, today and forever (Hebrews 13:8). And Jeremiah 1:12 says that He watches over His word to perform it! We are to be Christ like, we are Christ-men so our mouth, our attitudes and life style should reflect that of Jesus, being full of the Holy Spirit, going about doing good, conforming to and applying spiritual law that God set in motion in the beginning to govern all the affairs of this life. One such law is what many call the golden rule and is found in Matthew 7:12. Therefor all things whatsoever ye would that men should do to you, do ye even so to them: for this is the law and the prophets." Notice He did not say do unto others as they do to you but always treat others as you would want to be treated. If we follow this no matter how anyone responds to us or acts to us, His good will always come about. His goodness will follow us. If I am being good to someone that cusses me or mistreats me I am still to love them and operate according to this because I know even though the individual is acting that way, I have done my part and God will cause good to come. They may not come from that person but from somewhere else. He said in Galatians 6:7

that whatsoever a man sows he will reap. Always look for His goodness and mercy to follow you. It is a way of life, it is a life style!

The children of Israel wandered in the desert complaining for forty years and the word says they limited God (Psalm 78:40-43 KJ V). Let's not limit God, let's work with Him, living a life in His divine love, remembering all He has done and has promised yet to do and watch His goodness and mercy follow us! Pass it on to others, that passing it on is a real measure of appreciation of God's goodness and mercy to me. I will dwell in the house of the Lord forever!

What are some of the things David was saying? I know God is real and alive for I know Him. I have decided that I am His and He is mine and I am fully giving my life to Him. My heart is fixed on Him, there is no turning back. I will follow Him from now to eternity. I am fully content with Him and in Him and I have no desire to change. He is my life! God is with us 24 hours a day. We need to live as David did, with a full assurance and awareness of God's presence at all times in every situation and say with David, "Thou wilt show me the path of life: in Thy presence is the fullness of joy; and at Thy right hand are pleasures forever more. " (Psalm 17:11). We need to remember this Psalm was written from the stand point of the sheep, it is the flock or family of God. A house is not just a church building or sanctuary, it is the body of Christ. We are living stones built up to a spiritual house (I Peter 2:5). Being born again our bodies are the temple of the Holy Spirit (I Corinthians 3:16, 6:19-20). Reading Psalm 23:6 in the Amplified Bible makes reference to "the presence of the Lord forever."! Nothing can separate us from Him and His love (Romans 8:37-39). Knowing Jesus and who we are in Him gives a great sense of confidence and full trust. This is what we see all through this Psalm, confidence and full trust. This is abiding in Him from now through eternity! Dwell in His house, in His presence forever!

CONCLUSION

"According as His divine power hath given un to us all things that pertain unto life and godliness, Whereby are given unto us exceeding great and precious promises: that by these ye might be partakers of the divine nature, having escaped the corruption that is in the world through lust." II Peter 1:34 Our precious Lord and savior, the Great Shepherd of the sheep has made provision for everything that pertains to life and godliness. He left nothing undone, we must trust Him and walk out this life in Him conforming more to the image of Jesus every day and night in prayer searching His word, building up and growing up in His word and in Him. We must not look to our own understanding but in all our ways acknowledge Him and He will direct our ways just as promised in Proverbs 3:5-6. We need to cast all our care upon Him (Psalm 55:22 & I Peter 5:6-7).

We must live, walk, act and talk in His economy not ours or the worlds. He will never fail us or let us down! So in reflecting back through this Psalm we have been looking into, we saw that the Lord works in our behalf, He provides for us, He keeps us going, He guides us, He heals us and we will dwell in The house of the Lord forever! He has in this given us green pastures, clean still waters, guides us in new paths, protects us in dangerous places, frees us from fears and or worries and agitating passions, give antidotes for fly's and diseases which gives us a sound mind and a level head (II Timothy 1:7). He protects us from others. We can live everyday aware of His presence in us and around us. He is conscious of every circumstance that we encounter, I will continue from this moment throughout all eternity with Him because not even death can separate me from Him! That is why it is so very important to be growing daily in Him and His word and prayer getting to know Him more intimately daily, living and working with Him in everything we do. Getting to know and really understanding who we are in Christ Jesus for Colossians 1:26-27 says the mystery of God has been revealed and that is Christ in you your hope of glory!

We need to have a living and working knowledge of Him with us and in us at all times. This will produce a godly fear and deep reverence for our Lord that will change your life forever! Keep pressing in, keep confessing His word even when people or circumstances try discouraging you. Keep your eyes on Jesus and follow His lead, we must obey His word. Just as Jesus told them to roll away the stone on Lazarus' tomb and Martha the sister of Lazarus who was dead, said, "...by this time he stinketh ..." (John 11:39) and Jesus said in verse 40 "Said I not unto you, if thou wouldest believe thou shouldest see the glory of God?" They rolled away the stone, Jesus said in a loud voice "Lazarus come forth! "and he that was dead four days came forth alive! They unbound him from the grave cloths and he came out of the tomb alive! How many times do we question God like Martha did and go by what we see and feel instead of going by what the Lord has said? He has set us free from the bondages of the world, sin and death. Just believe God, find the promise and the answer to the problem in His word and take it to Him and believe Him for it, stand on His word. That is faith, you cannot worry in faith, it just cannot be done and it is impossible to please Him without faith (Hebrews 11:6).

That is why the children of Israel spent forty years in the wilderness and died in the wilderness without entering the promise land. They knew God's covenant promise of the land and believed that He promised it but they saw the giants in the land and doubt came in about them actually taking the land. God called it an evil report .(Nu.13:17- 14: we must not only know His word but also stand on His word and live by His word. The devil will tell you that you can't get out of this one but you have a choice, you can believe that or believe God and take Him at His word. It was the devil and or Martha's fleshly mind telling her that her brother Lazarus had been dead to long but Jesus resurrection life lifted him up and brought him forth out of that tomb alive! John 11:25 says that Jesus is the resurrection and the life! One word from the Master will bring the miracle working power of God to resurrect and bring life to any situation or thing in your life. Our greatest need is His greatest concern! So let's get to know Him more intimately every day.

When we know Him we will trust Him. We will know that the Lord is my Shepherd and I will not be in any want for anything! Revelation 1:8 says that He is the Alfa and Omega, the beginning and the end. Start with His word and end with His word, He must be first place in everything! Always speak positive according to His word, follow His lead continuously and live in victory! II Peter 1:3-4 says that He has given us all things that pertain to life and Godliness through His exceeding great and precious promises and that by these we might become partakers of His divine nature. His exceeding great and precious promises are found in His word, they are His word. The Lord has already made provision for all your needs (See also Mathew 6:33 and Philippians 4:19). We must know them in order to receive them and to receive them by faith.

Every area or subject we have touched on in this Psalm can be expounded on so much deeper and more exhaustive. I pray that what is written in this will stir up faith in you, encourage and in still an even deeper hunger for the Lord's word and presence and a desire to get to know Him more intimately. Jesus said in Mathew 5:6 that those who hunger and thirst after righteousness will be filled. And as Isaiah 12:3 puts it "Therefore with joy shall ye draw water out of the wells of salvation!" It gets more joyous the deeper and more intimate we get with our Lord. It would do well to study into the words salvation and saved in the old and new testaments. We are in our salvation and there are many benefits of it now as we approach our eternal, glorious state with Him! We have entered into life now if you are born again and it is life more abundant! (John 10:10 b).

To receive the promises, laid out in this book, you must get your mind, heart and mouth lined up with the Word of God. Heb.4:12 says that the Word of God is alive and powerful so we must do what Mark 11:23 says and speak to the situation. Speak the Word to your body. Speak the healing Scripture over your body. Do not speak the negative you see or feel. You have to build that inner image on the inside of you to line up with the Word of God! God is positive, not negative so you must learn to work with Him and not against Him in the positive attitude of His Word. You must receive these promises as you did your salvation. Receive them as a gift handed to you. Reach out and grab a hold of them! We have a covenant with God through the blood of Jesus and therefore have the blessings of Abraham according to Gal. 3! Study His Word and take it as God speaking directly to you because it is Him speaking directly to you!

In closing I will leave you with Hebrews 13:20-21 "Now the God of peace, that brought again from the dead our Lord Jesus, that Great Shepherd of the sheep, through the blood of the everlasting covenant, make you perfect in every good work to do His will, working in you that is well pleasing in His sight through Jesus Christ; to Whom be glory for ever and ever, Amen."

www.ingramcontent.com/pod-product-compliance
Lightning Source LLC
Chambersburg PA
CBHW030824060726

47590CB00004B/1390